Pinocchio

Retold by Sue Arengo
Illustrated by Damian Ward

OXFORD
UNIVERSITY PRESS

1 Before you read, what do you know about the story?

1 A carpenter made a girl out of wood.
☐ True ☑ False

2 Pinocchio planted his coin in a field.
☐ True ☐ False

3 Pinocchio changed into a donkey.
☐ True ☐ False

4 Pinocchio lied and his ears got longer.
☐ True ☐ False

5 Pinocchio became a real boy.
☐ True ☐ False

2 What are these animals? Which one is Pinocchio's friend?

c _ _ _ _ _ _
ecrtcki

d _ _ _ _ _ _
keyndo

w _ _ _ _ _
lawhe

ONCE there was an old man called Gepetto. He was poor and he lived alone in a small town near the sea.
Gepetto was a carpenter. He made things out of wood. One day Gepetto made a boy out of wood. He made a wooden puppet.

'I will call you Pinocchio!' said Gepetto.
'Put me down, Dad!' said the puppet.
'Oh!' said Gepetto. 'You can talk!'
'Of course I can!' said Pinocchio.
'Put me on the floor. I feel full of life and I want to dance.'
'Are you a good boy?' asked Gepetto.
'Of course I am!' said Pinocchio. 'I'm the best boy in the world!' Then he ran out of the door.

carpenter
a person who makes things from wood

floor
the ground of a building

wooden puppet

'Pinocchio, my son!' cried old Gepetto.
'Come back!'
The little puppet didn't listen. He just ran. But Gepetto
loved his son and so he ran after him.

'Come back!' shouted Gepetto. He tried to grab the
puppet but Pinocchio ran faster and faster. Gepetto
was old and could not catch him, and suddenly he
could not see him either.
'Puppet Boy, where are you?' Gepetto cried.

grab
take something
suddenly

Pinocchio ran back to Gepetto's room. But no one was there, because Gepetto was still out searching for him. Pinocchio was all alone and he was hungry, but there was no food. Then he heard a voice.

'Pinocchio! Look up!' There was a green cricket on the wall, with very bright eyes.

'Boys should be good to their parents,' it said. 'Good boys go to school and help people. But you're not a good boy. You're a bad wooden puppet!'

Then Pinocchio did another bad thing. He shouted at the cricket and chased it away. So now he was alone again.

chase
run after someone

cricket

search
look for something

voice
someone speaking

Pinocchio ran out into the dark street and knocked on someone's door.

'Oy! Be quiet!' shouted a man. 'What do you want?'

'Please, I want some bread!' said Pinocchio.

'Oh, do you?' said the man. 'Wait there.' He went inside, and then he came back to the window and poured a bucket of water all over Pinocchio.

'Here! Have a drink!' he said. 'Now go away or I'll throw the bucket at you too!'

Then Pinocchio began to cry. He was wet and cold and hungry. And he was all alone.

---

knock
hit lightly

Pinocchio ran back to Gepetto's room and fell asleep by the fire. Then his wooden feet got burnt.

When Gepetto came home, Pinocchio cried, 'Oh Dad! I'm sorry that I was a bad boy! Make me some new feet, Dad! And give me something to eat!'

Gepetto wanted to be angry. But then he saw Pinocchio's poor burnt feet.

'My poor boy!' he said. And he gave him all the food he had – three hard green pears. Pinocchio was so hungry he ate them all.

burnt
so hot that they
were on fire

pear

1 Choose the correct word.

1 Gepetto was a ... He made things out of wood.

   a ☐ puppet   b ☑ carpenter   c ☐ boy

2 'I am the best boy in the ...,' said Pinocchio.

   a ☐ world   b ☐ town   c ☐ sea

3 Gepetto shouted, 'Come back!' But Pinocchio didn't ...

   a ☐ listen   b ☐ cry   c ☐ run

4 In Gepetto's room there was a green ... on the wall.

   a ☐ bucket   b ☐ cricket   c ☐ pear

5 'Good boys go to school and ... people,' said the cricket.

   a ☐ catch   b ☐ chase   c ☐ help

6 Pinocchio knocked on someone's door because he wanted ...

   a ☐ water   b ☐ bread   c ☐ Gepetto

7 Pinocchio began to ... because he was wet and hungry.

   a ☐ shout   b ☐ run   c ☐ cry

8 Pinocchio's wooden feet got ... by the fire.

   a ☐ burnt   b ☐ cold   c ☐ bright

9 Pinocchio was sorry that he was ...

   a ☐ wet   b ☐ angry   c ☐ bad

10 Gepetto gave Pinocchio three green ...

   a ☐ pears   b ☐ apples   c ☐ crickets

2 Complete the story with the words.

~~alone~~   bad   burnt   good   hard   hungry

old   poor   small   sorry   wet   wooden

Gepetto lived [1] _____alone_____ in a [2] _____ town near the sea. One day he made a [3] _____ puppet. He made a boy and he called him Pinocchio.

Pinocchio ran out of the door. 'Come back, Pinocchio!' shouted Gepetto. He tried to catch his son, but Gepetto was [4] _____ and Pinocchio ran faster.

Pinocchio was alone and [5] _____. A green cricket told Pinocchio, 'Boys should be [6] _____ to their parents. But you're a [7] _____ wooden puppet.'

The man poured a bucket of water all over Pinocchio. Now he was [8] _____ , hungry and alone.

Pinocchio slept by the fire and his feet got [9] _____.
When Gepetto came home, Pinocchio said he was [10] _____. Gepetto said, 'My [11] _____ boy!' and gave him three [12] _____ pears to eat.

3 What happens next? Choose one sentence.

1 ☐ Pinocchio finds some money.

2 ☐ Pinocchio goes to the sea.

3 ☐ Pinocchio gets a writing book.

4 ☐ Pinocchio tells a lie.

Gepetto made Pinocchio some new feet and the little puppet hugged him.

'Listen,' said Gepetto. 'You must go to school. I want you to work hard and be a good boy.'

'But I can't go to school without a writing book,' said Pinocchio.

'Wait there,' said Gepetto. 'I'll get one.'

When Gepetto returned, Pinocchio said, 'Where's your coat, Dad?' Gepetto didn't answer. He just said, 'Look! Here's your writing book!'

'Oh Dad!' said Pinocchio. 'You sold your coat to buy my book, didn't you? I'll be a good boy. I'll go to school tomorrow.'

hug

But on his way to school, Pinocchio saw something.

'Two pence,' said a man. 'It only costs two pence to see the famous puppets dance.'

'I'm going to school,' said Pinocchio. 'And I don't have any money.'

'Hey!' said the man. 'Go to school tomorrow. I'll give you two pence for that writing book. Come and see the dancing puppets!'

It did sound interesting so Pinocchio said, 'OK.'

But the puppets stopped dancing when they saw Pinocchio.

'Hey! Puppet boy!' they shouted. 'Come and dance with us!'

Then everyone in the audience turned and looked at him.

audience
the people watching
a show

9

Then the nasty Puppet Master arrived. 'Why aren't you puppets dancing?' he shouted. 'And who's this?' he asked, looking at Pinocchio.

The puppets were so afraid that they could not move.

'OK!' shouted the Puppet Master. 'Time for bed!'

'But first I need some wood for the fire. I want to cook my dinner!'

He grabbed an old puppet. 'Ah! Here's some wood!' he laughed.

Then Pinocchio did something brave.

'Let him go!' he cried. 'Put that puppet down!'

afraid	brave	nasty
feeling fear	not afraid of danger	mean

'Take me!' he shouted bravely. 'Put me on your fire and let this old puppet go!'

'What?' said the Puppet Master. 'What did you say?'

The Puppet Master could not understand why Pinocchio was not afraid. He looked at Pinocchio's eyes. Pinocchio's eyes were not afraid.

Suddenly the Puppet Master felt tired. He dropped the old wooden puppet onto the floor. 'OK,' he said. 'No more dancing today. You can all go to bed.'

1 What do they say? Order the words.

1 Gepetto: | want you | to work | I | hard | . |
| a good boy | and be |

I want you to work hard and be a good boy.

2 Pinocchio: | your coat | my book, | You | to buy |
| didn't you | ? | sold |

_____

3 Man: | to see | . | It | two pence | dance |
| only costs | the famous puppets |

_____

4 Man: | . | two pence | give you | I'll |
| for | writing book | that |

_____

5 Puppet Master: | the fire | I | for | First |
| some wood | need | . |

_____

6 Pinocchio: | go | on your fire | ! | Put me |
| let | and | this old puppet |

_____

2 Complete the sentences. Then act the play.

audience   bed   dinner   fire   pence   ~~puppets~~

school   wood

Man   Come and see the famous dancing ¹_*puppets*_!
                   It only costs two ²_____.

Pinocchio   I'm going to ³_____.

Man   Go to school tomorrow. Come on! Come and see
                   the famous puppets dance.

Pinocchio   OK. It sounds interesting.
                   The puppets stopped dancing and everyone in the
                   ⁴_____ *turned and looked at Pinocchio.*

Puppet Master I want to cook my ⁵_____ and I need
                   some ⁶_____ for the fire.

Pinocchio   Put him down! Let that old wooden puppet go!
                   Take me and put me on your ⁷_____!

Puppet Master I feel tired. No more dancing today. You can all
                   go to ⁸_____.

3 What happens next? Choose.

	Yes	No
1 Pinocchio stays with the Puppet Master.	☐	☐
2 Pinocchio buys a coat for Gepetto.	☐	☐
3 Pinocchio meets some bad boys.	☐	☐
4 Pinocchio loses his hat.	☐	☐

In the morning, the Puppet Master spoke to Pinocchio. 'Where do you come from?' he asked.

'My father's a poor old carpenter,' said Pinocchio. 'He sold his coat to buy me a writing book. But I sold that book to see your puppet show. I was bad, but I want to be good now.'

'You're an interesting ... thing,' said the Puppet Master. 'And brave. Here ... take these coins. Give them to your father. Now go! Quick! Or I might keep you.'

'Oh! Thanks, Mr Puppet Master,' said Pinocchio. Then he grabbed the coins and ran.

coin

Pinocchio walked home through the town. On the way, he met the Fox brothers.

'Hello, Pinocchio,' said Tommy Fox. 'What are you doing?'

'I'm going home,' said Pinocchio. 'I've got five coins! So I'm going to buy a new coat for my dad! And a writing book, because I need to go to school.'

'Forget about the coat,' said Danny Fox. 'Winter will be over soon.'

'And you don't need school,' said Tommy Fox. 'You need to go into business. Listen! There's a magic field outside the town. Plant your coins there and they will grow into money trees. Each one will have a thousand coins shining in the sunlight!'

'Wow!' said Pinocchio.

business	magic	shine
making money		

'But first, let's eat,' said Tommy Fox. And he took them to a restaurant.

'Waiter!' shouted Danny Fox. 'Twenty ducks with hot cream!'

'And I'll have twenty chickens in hot butter!' said Tommy Fox.

'And you?' the waiter asked Pinocchio.

'Er ...' said Pinocchio. 'Do you have any pears?'

'Not today,' said the waiter.

'Then just some bread and cheese for me, please,' said Pinocchio.

At the end of the meal, the Fox brothers said, 'We're just going to wash our hands and then we'll pay the bill.'

But they never came back. So Pinocchio had to pay for the meal. Then he only had one coin left.

pay
give someone
money

restaurant
a place where we
buy and eat food

the bill

waiter
a man who works
in a restaurant

Outside, it was dark. Pinocchio started to walk and then he saw the cricket again.

'Pinocchio!' said the cricket. It looked at him with bright eyes. 'Coins don't grow into trees!'

'I haven't got any coins!' lied Pinocchio. And when he told this lie, his nose suddenly got longer.

Just then two robbers grabbed Pinocchio.

'Give us your money!' they cried.

'I haven't got any money!' lied Pinocchio. And his nose grew longer again.

'What's wrong with your nose?' said the robbers. Pinocchio hid the coin in his mouth.

'It's in his mouth!' shouted the robbers. They grabbed him and held him upside down.

'Drop it, Big Nose!' they shouted. But Pinocchio kept his mouth shut.

---

grow
get bigger

robber
a person who
steals things

tell a lie
not tell the truth

1 Read and match.

1 Gepetto made a boy out of wood ...

2 Gepetto ran after Pinocchio ...

3 Pinocchio began to cry because ...

4 Gepetto made Pinocchio some new feet ...

5 Gepetto sold his old coat and ...

6 Pinocchio gave his writing book to the man ...

7 When the dancing puppets saw Pinocchio, ...

8 The Puppet Master wanted some wood ...

9 The Fox brothers told Pinocchio ...

10 The Fox brothers took Pinocchio to a restaurant, ...

a but Pinocchio paid the bill.

b to make a fire and cook his dinner.

c he was hungry and all alone.

d they stopped dancing and looked at him.

e but Pinocchio was faster.

f and called him Pinocchio.

g bought his son a writing book.

h to plant his coins in a magic field.

i because his feet got burnt by the fire.

j so that he could see the dancing puppets.

2 What did they say? Write the names.

Tommy Fox   Danny Fox   ~~Pinocchio~~   the cricket

Pinocchio   the robbers   the Fox brothers   Pinocchio

1 I'm going to buy a new coat for my dad. ____Pinocchio____

2 Forget the coat. Winter will be over
   soon. _____

3 Plant your coins in the magic field and
   they will grow into money trees. _____

4 Just some bread and cheese, please. _____

5 We're going to wash our hands and
   then we'll pay the bill. _____

6 Coins don't grow into trees. _____

7 I haven't got any coins! _____

8 Give us your money! _____

A kind lady came to help Pinocchio and took him to her home.

'Hello, Pinocchio. I'm a friend and I saw it all!' she said. 'Those robbers were trying to steal your money.'

'Money?' said Pinocchio. 'What money?' And his nose grew longer again!

'They wanted your money,' said the Kind Friend. 'Where is it now?'

'Under the tree,' lied Pinocchio. Really it was in his hand. So many lies! Again his nose got longer.

'Your nose is growing,' smiled the Friend. 'You're lying.'

'I'm not!' said Pinocchio. And his nose grew longer again. Suddenly Pinocchio's nose was as long as the bed!

'Listen,' said the Kind Friend. 'Stop telling lies!'

So then he showed her his coin, and at once his nose was perfectly alright again.

steal
take someone
else's things

'Now don't tell any more lies!' said the Friend kindly.

'Be good, and go and find your father.'

So Pinocchio thanked her and hurried back to town.

But then ... Oh no! He met the Fox brothers again!

'Ah!' said Tommy Fox. 'Where did you go? And where is the money?'

Pinocchio didn't want to tell a lie so he showed them the coin.

'Now!' said Danny Fox. 'Let's plant it in the magic field.'

'No,' said Pinocchio. 'I don't want to.'

'Look!' said Tommy Fox. 'Here's the magic field!'

Pinocchio saw an ordinary field.

'Come on!' said Tommy Fox.

---

ordinary
not special

'Dig a hole!' said Tommy Fox.
'Plant your coin!' said Danny Fox.
'Just think! Soon you'll be rich! But first you need to water that coin! So go and fetch some water.'
Pinocchio fetched some water and came back.
He waited and waited, but nothing happened. Then he saw the cricket again. The cricket looked at him and said, 'Pinocchio! They took your money!'
Then Pinocchio looked in the hole and saw that it was empty.

dig
make a hole in the ground

empty
when there is nothing there

fetch
go and get

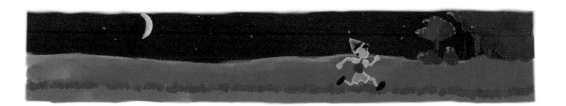

It was the middle of the night. Pinocchio ran up the road. He wanted to find the Kind Friend again and speak to her.

But Pinocchio couldn't find the Kind Friend's cottage. He could only find a big stone. And Pinocchio thought that she might be dead. So he started to cry. Suddenly, a large white bird appeared.

'Come with me, Pinocchio!' it said. 'I will carry you to the sea. Your father's looking for you. He's in a little boat.'

So Pinocchio got on the bird's back, and they flew away.

---

cottage
a small house

1 Read and match.

1 Pinocchio told lots of lies ...

2 Pinocchio showed his friend the coin ...

3 The Kind Friend told Pinocchio to ...

4 Pinocchio hurried back to town ...

5 Pinocchio showed the Fox brothers his coin and ...

6 The Fox brothers told Pinocchio ...

7 Pinocchio went to fetch some water ...

8 Pinocchio looked in the hole ...

9 Pinocchio thought that the Kind Friend ...

10 A large bird came ...

a they took him to a magic field.

b and met the Fox brothers.

c but it was empty.

d and his nose was perfectly alright again.

e and soon his nose was as long as the bed.

f and Pinocchio flew away with it.

g and the Fox brothers stole his coin.

h to plant the coin.

i be good and go and find his father.

j might be dead.

2 Write the words.

7▾

1▾

2▾ a man who
works in a
restaurant

	1 m			8▸		▸3				2			4

1 m
a
g
i
6 c

3▾

3▸ look for something

5

9▸ make a hole in
the ground

▸8

7

4▾

▸9   10   ▸11

5▾ not afraid of
danger

▸12

10▾ get bigger

6▸ a person who makes
things from wood

11▸

12▸ a person who steals things

3 What happens next? Choose.

	Yes	No
1 Pinocchio and Gepetto go home.	☐	☐
2 Pinocchio meets the Kind Friend again.	☐	☐
3 Pinocchio goes to school.	☐	☐
4 Pinocchio changes into a real boy.	☐	☐

They came to the sea and the wind was strong. Pinocchio saw Gepetto in a little boat.
'Father!' he cried. 'Dad!'
His father looked up and saw him. And then, suddenly, he fell into the water.

'Dad!' shouted Pinocchio. 'I will help you!' And bravely he jumped into the sea. The waves were big and Pinocchio went up and down all day. But he couldn't find his father. Some hours later, the water carried Pinocchio to an island.

waves

Pinocchio lay on the sand. He was tired, lonely and hungry – but he was alive.

After a while he got up. He saw people working. Two men were making baskets.

'Hello!' said Pinocchio. 'Can you give me some bread?'

'You have to work for your food here,' they said.

Another man was mending a net. 'Do you know how to mend nets?' he said.

'Er ...' said Pinocchio.

Then an old woman said, 'Help me carry this bucket of water and I'll cook something for you.' Pinocchio didn't want to carry the bucket. But he was very hungry.

alive	mend	net
not dead	fix something	something we use to catch fish

The bucket was very heavy. But Pinocchio carried it all the way to the old woman's house.

'Thank you,' she said. And she cooked something nice for him.

Then Pinocchio saw her blue hair. 'It's you!' he cried. 'The Kind Friend!'

'Yes,' she said.

'But you're different!'

'Yes. I am older now.'

'Will I grow older?' asked Pinocchio.

'No,' she said. 'Puppets can't grow. Only real boys can grow.'

Then Pinocchio started to cry. 'I want to be a real boy! I don't want to be a wooden puppet!'

'If you go to school and work hard,' she said, 'then you will become a real boy.'

So the next day Pinocchio went to school.

'Oh!' shouted the school bullies. 'A puppet!'

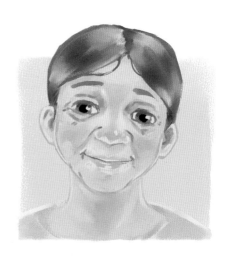

'You can't learn anything, Wooden Head!' said a boy. But Pinocchio didn't listen to them. He worked hard. He listened to the teacher. He didn't talk in class. And he made friends with a boy called Candlewick. The Kind Friend was pleased with him.

'Tomorrow evening you'll be a real boy!' she said.

bullies
mean, unfriendly people

1 Answer the questions.

1 What happened when Pinocchio jumped into the sea?

a ☑ He couldn't find his father.

b ☐ He jumped into his father's boat.

2 Where did the sea carry Pinocchio to?

a ☐ An island.　　b ☐ Gepetto's house.

3 What was the man mending?

a ☐ A bucket.　　b ☐ A net.

4 Why did Pinocchio carry the bucket?

a ☐ To help an old woman.

b ☐ To help the man.

5 Who did Pinocchio meet again on the island?

a ☐ The cricket.　　b ☐ The Kind Friend.

6 Why did Pinocchio cry?

a ☐ Because he wanted to go to school.

b ☐ Because he wanted to be a real boy.

7 What did Pinocchio do at school?

a ☐ He worked hard.

b ☐ He listened to the bullies.

2 Write *was*, *wasn't*, *were* or *weren't*.

1 Pinocchio's father _____*was*_____ in the water.

2 The waves _____ small.

3 Pinocchio _____ tired and hungry.

4 The people on the island _____ working.

5 A man _____ mending a net.

6 The bucket of water _____ easy to carry.

7 The old woman's hair _____ red.

8 The Kind Friend _____ pleased with Pinocchio.

9 The bullies _____ kind to Pinocchio.

10 Pinocchio _____ good and worked hard in school.

3 What does Pinocchio see next? Tick the boxes.

1 ☐

2 ☐

3 ☐

4 ☐

5 ☐

6 ☐

But the next day Candlewick said, 'Hey, Pinocchio. I'm not going to school today. I'm going to Lazyland.'

'What's that?' said Pinocchio.

'It's a fun place,' said Candlewick. 'Nobody does any work. There are no teachers. We just play and eat sweets all day.'

Then a very strange bus arrived. It was pulled by eight grey donkeys.

'Come on,' said Candlewick.

The bus did look interesting, so Pinocchio said, 'OK.'

'You'll be sorry!' said one of the donkeys. 'I was a boy like you once!'

donkey

Lazyland was a noisy place. There were children everywhere, playing and shouting and eating sweets. It was fun at first, but soon Pinocchio felt tired and wanted to go home.

'Oh, come on,' said Candlewick. 'Have some more sweets!'

The next day Pinocchio felt strange.

'Ah!' he cried. 'Candlewick! Help! My ears! Oh no! Your ears are the same!'

'We've got the donkey sickness!' said Candlewick. 'We are changing into donkeys.'

It was true. Soon they had tails and fur. Then the bus driver took them to a donkey market and sold them.

fur
hairy skin
like animals have

sweets

An angry man bought Pinocchio, but soon he didn't want him any more.

'I'm going to throw this donkey into the sea and get a new one,' he said.

Pinocchio fell into the deep blue water. And slowly he changed back into a puppet. Then a huge whale opened its mouth and suddenly Pinocchio found himself inside. There he could breathe ... and there inside the whale he saw ... his father!

'Dad!' he cried. 'I tried to help you!'

'There's nothing to eat but fish,' said the old man. 'How can we get out of here?'

'The way we came in,' said Pinocchio. 'Let's go!'

When the whale opened its mouth, they swam out. Then a dolphin carried them back to land.

breathe
let air in and out
of your mouth

dolphin

whale

Now Gepetto was too old and tired to work, so
Pinocchio took him home. Pinocchio went back to
school.

'You are a good boy, Pinocchio,' Gepetto said.

'But I'm not a boy, Dad,' said Pinocchio. 'I'm just a wooden
puppet!'

Pinocchio worked hard. Every day he went to school and
listened to his teacher, and at night he helped Gepetto.
Together they cooked their evening meal
and talked about Pinocchio's day at school.
The Kind Friend was getting old too, so
Pinocchio took food to her and helped her
carry buckets of water.

Some time later, Pinocchio had a dream. The Kind Friend spoke to him.

'Pinocchio!' she said. 'You are brave! And now you are also kind. You work hard and you are good. Because of this you are changing. Your heart is now a real heart. One day you will be a real man. Pinocchio! You are not a puppet any more! You are a real boy!'

And when Pinocchio woke up ... he saw that it was true!

---

dream
pictures in your head
when you are asleep

heart

1 Number the sentences to tell the story.

☐ Gepetto sold his coat.

☐ Pinocchio and the Fox brothers went to a restaurant.

☐ Pinocchio found his father inside a whale.

[1] Gepetto made a boy out of wood – a puppet.

☐ Pinocchio sold his writing book to see the famous dancing puppets.

☐ Pinocchio dreamed that he was real, and in the morning he woke up and found that it was true.

☐ Two robbers tried to steal Pinocchio's money.

☐ Pinocchio went to Lazyland with Candlewick and they both turned into donkeys.

☐ A white bird carried Pinocchio to the sea.

☐ Pinocchio jumped into the sea to help his father.

☐ Pinocchio lied and his nose grew longer.

☐ Pinocchio carried a bucket for an old lady and she cooked him some food.

☐ Pinocchio fell asleep by the fire and burnt his feet.

☐ Pinocchio worked hard at school and helped the Kind Friend.

☐ The Puppet Master gave Pinocchio five coins.

OXFORD
UNIVERSITY PRESS

Great Clarendon Street, Oxford OX2 6DP

Oxford University Press is a department of the University of Oxford.
It furthers the University's objective of excellence in research, scholarship,
and education by publishing worldwide in

Oxford New York

Auckland Cape Town Dar es Salaam Hong Kong Karachi
Kuala Lumpur Madrid Melbourne Mexico City Nairobi
New Delhi Shanghai Taipei Toronto

With offices in

Argentina Austria Brazil Chile Czech Republic France
Greece Guatemala Hungary Italy Japan Poland Portugal
Singapore South Korea Switzerland Thailand Turkey
Ukraine Vietnam

OXFORD and OXFORD ENGLISH are registered trade marks
of Oxford University Press in the UK and in certain other
countries

© Oxford University Press 2009

The moral rights of the author have been asserted

Database right Oxford University Press (maker)

First published 2009

2020 2019 2018 2017 2016
16   15   14   13   12

ISBN: 978 0 19 480263 5

Printed in China

This book is printed on paper from certified and well-managed sources.

ACKNOWLEDGEMENTS
Original story retold by: Sue Arengo
Illustrated by: Damian Ward/Tugeau 2 Inc.